THE
COUNCIL
OF EQUALS

A Guide and Handbook
for Shared Governance

by
George SanFacon

Cover art, text layout and graphic design by:
Alex SanFaçon
email: alexsanfacon@gmail.com
phone: 773-206-4215

Published by:
Charing Cross Press
P.O. Box 6052
Ann Arbor, MI 48106-6052
email: HLRideas@umich.edu
phone: 734-971-3455

Copies of this book can be ordered from Charing Cross Press at a cost of $25 (includes handling and postage) or online at www.amazon.com.

Printed in the United States of America.

ISBN: 978-0-9826320-8-6

Dedication

To those who joined me in walking the council path, especially Roy Christian, Ken Davis, Vicky Hueter, Joe Kennedy, and Jeff Schroeder.

And to those who brought us the wisdom to make it work, especially Barb Cecil, John DeSouza, Bernadette Malinoski, and Anita Zimmerman.

Table of Contents ⸺

IV. Handling Road Bumps

V. Getting Started

VI. Appendices

Introduction _____

Greetings.

What follows is my attempt to create a simple and practical guide for a *council of equals,* a group of people using consensus decision making to govern and manage an enterprise. What kind of group? Any kind — a team in the workplace, a volunteer association, a board of trustees, or a government cabinet. What kind of enterprise? Any kind — formal or informal, big or small, public or private, for-profit or non-profit.

Participants and observers are invariably surprised and impressed with both the effectiveness and sense of basic goodness engendered by shared governance and the council experience. They often wonder, therefore, about the possibility of using it elsewhere in their lives. So I occasionally get requests to write something that would help support that. Well, here it is. And hopefully, folks will find a lot of what they need to know for getting started and using this life-giving approach for joint endeavors. It includes an overview of basic concepts, working definitions and related understandings, charts and graphics to underscore key concepts, as well as practices and guidelines for making things work where the rubber meets the road. There is also a listing of field-tested complementary resources for those who choose to take the adventure further.

These are not the abstract musings and speculations of an armchair theoretician, but rather the insights and learning gained from my own, direct lived experience. I have collaborated with others on councils for over three decades in a variety of capacities and settings. In some of those venues, I was held personally accountable for the results, thereby placing my career and livelihood on the line. But rest assured, the outcomes have been wonderful and I am still here walking the planet and having fun. So what follows could have relevance and possibility for you.

There is a lot of business and organizational jargon herein. I have used it to help those in formal leadership positions see the possibilities for applying the model in their organizational and institutional settings. Nevertheless, the concepts are universal and can be applied in the broadest sense; that is, by any group of two or more people working together on common goals—from a couple raising a family to a company manufacturing a product.

But be forewarned: the council of equals is subversive. What do I mean by subversive? I mean that what is experienced using it undermines the credibility and legitimacy of autocratic top-down approaches. After living out loud in such a framework, people have a hard time going back to the old way of doing things. But that shouldn't be much of a surprise. After all, autocratic approaches are based on fear—emphasizing control, domination, and manipulation, whereas participatory approaches are based on love—emphasizing partnership, transparency, and authenticity. Since this is a hands-on guide, I have not included much information on the limits and drawbacks of the former. Nor have I included a lot of data and arguments to convince skeptics of the relative superiority of the latter. If you are interested in such, I invite you to check out some of the resources and references cited in the back of the book. For our purposes here, however, it is enough to state the following:

> *Participatory approaches done well almost always*
> *result in higher levels of productivity and effectiveness.*
> *That is because they evoke higher levels of trust,*
> *morale, energy, and commitment—intangibles of the*
> *human spirit.*

People in formal leadership positions often think of themselves as stewards of the status quo, which is appropriate. After all, our society and its many benefits are part and parcel of what came before, so preservation and continuity are incredibly important. But things are admittedly unfinished in our society; there is much yet that needs to be changed and improved upon, including our systems of governance and management. And only designated leaders are formally vested with the power to change them. So unless there is a revolution, it is up to them—as individuals and one at a time—to decide whether or not to adopt a council of equals approach for whatever part of the system they are in charge of and held accountable for.

Fortunately, a council can work almost anywhere, even within a larger autocratic organization. It is not necessary for the greater system to embrace the concept in order for individual leaders and their teams to successfully adopt and use it. As long as there is at least neutral regard for it in the larger system, rather than outright hostility, the council approach can work.

Lastly, the wellspring of wisdom and know-how for successfully using the council of equals lies ever present within you. You only have to open to and listen for the quiet voice within, which is often drowned out by the din and clamor of myopic ego and mainstream culture. Indeed, this wellspring is part of your most essential self and, as the sages say, "closer to you than your own breath." It manifests there as a yearning and intention to bring basic goodness to your endeavors with others—wherever and with whomever they may be—no matter what. May what follows herein support the expression of that ineffable impulse through the spirit and form of council.

George

Bahia Honda State Park
Big Pine Key, Florida
September 2014

I. Basic Concepts

Freedom is participation in power.

~Cicero

Governance

Governance is about having and exercising authority over an organization or a group. Standard texts and dictionaries inform us that it encompasses the right to:

- establish strategic direction
- make policy
- administer affairs
- command others
- exact obedience

Because it encompasses these executive functions, governance is the metasystem of an enterprise, through which all the other systems are mediated and controlled. It is also about the way we distribute power, rights, and responsibilities; in other words, the way we choose to live together. And these choices can generally be classified as either *autocratic* or *participatory*.

Autocratic systems are based on exercising power over others. These approaches are exclusive: one person has the ability to force others to do things they may or may not want to do. Leaders focus on command and control. And the underlying motivational energy is fear. The central issue in autocratic systems is how the people at the top can hold and exercise power over others without ultimately sharing it.

governance

having and exercising authority over an organization or a group

having the right to:
establish strategic direction, make policy, administer affairs, command others, and exact obedience

Participatory systems, on the other hand, are based on sharing power with others. These approaches are reciprocal: each person is able to influence and be influenced by others in deciding what they choose to do and support. Leaders focus on partnership and mutuality. And the underlying motivational energy is love. The central issue in participatory systems is how people can be open and vulnerable to one another while still meeting their own personal needs for well-being and selfhood.

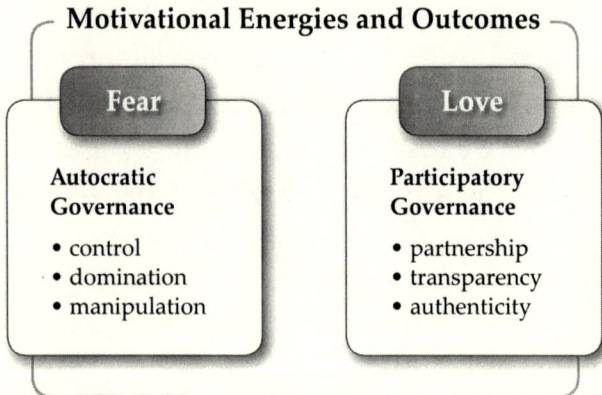

Motivational Energies and Outcomes

Fear

Autocratic Governance

- control
- domination
- manipulation

Love

Participatory Governance

- partnership
- transparency
- authenticity

For over three thousand years, the prevailing forms of governance have been autocratic. But during the past few centuries, people have been moving toward more participatory ones. This trend has resulted in our democratic government, the prohibition of slavery, and progress toward the emancipation of women. We are living in a period of transition—a crossover time—from exercising power over to sharing power with.

Participatory Governance

is about ... *sharing power with*

rather than ... *exercising power over*

Management

The purpose of *management* is to combine and connect various actions and efforts into an integrated whole: one that effectively accomplishes the goals of the enterprise. It is common to all types of endeavors, is found at all organizational levels, and needs to be done whether people choose to govern through autocracy or participation. The work of management generally includes:

Framing. Identifying and clarifying the governing ideas of the enterprise, including its purpose, mission, values, and goals.

Planning. Forecasting and anticipating the future, determining the appropriate activities for the enterprise, and then allocating resources.

Organizing. Structuring and allocating work, including the responsibilities and levels of authority.

Staffing. Selecting, training, and developing people.

Decision Making. Choosing a course of action from available alternatives.

Facilitating. Supporting and enhancing the performance of people in accomplishing the goals.

Controlling. Measuring and evaluating outcomes, then guiding or correcting efforts toward accomplishing the goals.

These management functions comprise the shirtsleeve work of leadership: translating visions and goals into actions and reality. This handbook and guide is about how a group can get the management work done through participatory governance—a council of equals.

Accountability

In formal organizations, designated leaders—such as supervisors, owners, executive officers, CEOs, trustees, bosses, managers, directors, principals, superintendents, and the like—are held *accountable.* They are thereby obliged to provide a reckoning on group performance and outcomes, for what their assigned group does or does not do, for what does or does not happen. This accountability entails a potential liability and risk for which the leader may be personally called to account.

Because of this risk, leaders are usually reluctant to share real power with others. And that is natural: most of us want to control things when we are personally at risk for the outcomes. For that reason, top-down approaches are the norm in our organizations, businesses, and institutions. But participatory approaches generally outperform autocratic ones. So it is ironic that in making the choice that feels safest, leaders most often choose the approach that places themselves and the enterprise at greater risk. Besides generating a sense of control and safety for leaders, there is another reason for the preponderance of autocratic systems in our society: it is what we know. Throughout our lives, most of us were raised and socially conditioned in autocratic systems—from family, to school, to work.

> **accountable**
>
> 1. being expected to provide a reckoning for what does or does not happen, and
>
> 2. being personally at risk for such

Participatory Approaches

With any polarity—such as *hot versus cold* and *full versus empty*—there is an infinite number of possibilities on the spectrum between the two extremes. So it is with *autocratic versus participatory* governance. Nevertheless, there are several distinct neighborhoods that can be identified along the spectrum, as shown in the chart on the following page.

Neighborhoods of Governance

participatory

consensus

voting

consultative

benevolent autocratic

exploitive autocratic

autocratic

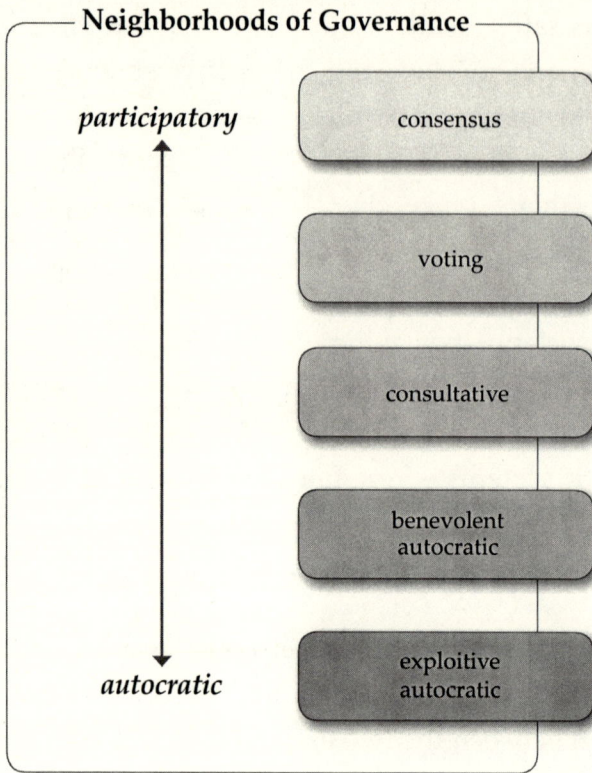

At the participatory end of the spectrum—where power is shared—the options for governance are:

Consultative. Control of the enterprise is held by a person in charge or designated leader. He or she unilaterally makes the major decisions, though there are opportunities for group members to influence those decisions beforehand.

Voting. Control of the enterprise is held by the group as a whole. Major decisions are made by the group on the basis of voting; the majority makes the decisions and issues orders that the minority must follow.

Consensus. Control of the enterprise is held by the group as a whole. Major decisions are made on the basis of consensus, and each member of the group has the power to block any specific decision.

These options entail increasing levels of participation and power sharing, as depicted in the following chart.

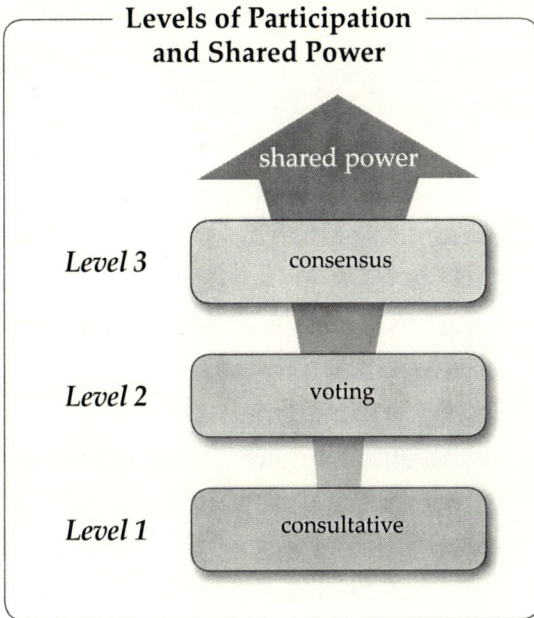

Levels of Participation and Shared Power

shared power

Level 3 — consensus

Level 2 — voting

Level 1 — consultative

Thus, leaders have three basic options for sharing power with others in their group. They can: (1) ask others for their opinions and then unilaterally (on their own) decide what to do; (2) have everyone vote and abide by the majority; or (3) use consensus. Let's look further at each of these.

The first option—consultative—isn't really sharing much power at all. The leader asks others for their opinions, which may or may not be of any influence, then decides and tells others what to do.

The second option—voting—is often assumed to be the most participatory approach, probably because of our democratic government and political system. But consider the working definition of autocracy: exercising power over. In voting, the majority exercises power over the minority. Thus, voting entails a form of coercion, whereby the majority makes the decision and forces the minority to do or support something they do not want. But it has other drawbacks as well. First, a leader could be held personally accountable for a group decision that he or she opposed in being part of the minority. Given the number of decisions that need to be made in organizations and the myriad things that can go wrong, it would be foolish for a leader to adopt such a framework, giving up control and placing his or her livelihood and career at such risk. Second, voting creates winners (the majority) and losers (the minority) within the group, which leads to factions. These subgroups coalesce out of the interplay of differing worldviews and personal affinities within the win/lose context of majority rule. Lastly, voting results in the wisdom of the minority being lost: overruled and obliterated by the majority.

That leaves us with the third option—consensus.

Consensus

Consensus is a decision and state of mutual agreement by all members of a group, rather than a majority or just the boss. But this agreement does not mean conformity, in which everyone thinks alike (commonly referred to as *groupthink*). It simply means that the proposed decision or action is acceptable to and can be supported by each of the members.

Consensus means that every member is willing to accept and support a decision as a good one for the group, even if it is not their personal first choice. For complicated or controversial issues, consensus is usually reached after: (1) each individual has had the opportunity to express his or her concerns, and (2) those concerns have been understood and considered by the group. The underlying goal of the consensus process is to create unity while valuing diversity.

> **consensus**
>
> every member in the group accepts and supports the proposed decision or action, even if it is not their personal first choice

In classic consensus, each and every member must consent to a decision before the group can adopt it. In other words, each member has the power to *block* a decision by the group, thereby preventing it from being made. By exercising that power, an individual is stating that he or she believes the proposed decision is so seriously wrong that the group should not be allowed to proceed with it. As long as a proposed decision is blocked, the status quo prevails.

But not all groups that practice consensus do so in this classic sense. The most common variants are:

Consensus-Minus-One. In this approach, a decision is ratified if all but one person consents to it. So it takes at least two members to block a decision.

The Quaker Method. Here the group strives to arrive at "a general sense of the meeting" after due deliberation and discussion. This sense is a statement of what is perceived to be the best possible decision for the group at that particular time. Action is taken when the group can proceed "in substantial unity."

Stepping Aside. In this approach (which may be adopted in conjunction with either of the preceding variants), if all are in agreement but one or two individuals, they are asked whether or not they would be willing to step aside. By stepping aside, the individuals are saying: "We do not agree with the decision, but do not feel that it is wrong and that it would be better for the group to adopt it than do nothing at all." It also means that while they are willing to have the decision go forward, they do not want to take part in carrying it out.

While these approaches vary from the classic model, they each emphasize: (1) understanding the different perspectives, (2) taking all concerns into consideration, and (3) striving to find the most universally acceptable decision possible at a particular time. And they all intend to arrive at the same place: a decision or solution that everyone can support. When that happens, everyone can feel it.

The consensus model proposed and explained herein for a council of equals is a classic one. Nevertheless, what follows is equally relevant to the common variants.

While consensus decision making is rare in organizational governance, it is common in our everyday life. It shows up wherever people are in *right relationship* with one another; that is, wherever care and consideration are truly extended to those present. Couples, for example, might use consensus to decide which movie to watch or where to go on vacation. They might also use it for bigger fish, such as deciding whether or not to get married. Because consensus is part of a larger dynamic within right relationship, we tend not to see or distinguish it as such. But it is there, quietly weaving us together and enriching our lives: a natural expression of love and the ineffable goodheartedness that lies deep within us.

There are several advantages to using consensus. First, it extends respect and consideration to others by including them in decisions that affect them. Each person is encouraged to show up, share his or her perspective, and be heard. And each one has the power to either consent to or block a decision. Because the decisions have to be acceptable to a variety of people and thereby meet a wide range of requirements, they tend to be workable and effective as well as imaginative and creative. The resulting synthesis is often better than any of the originally competing ideas. Moreover, with consensus there are no losers (as with voting) or subordinates (as with a boss) grudgingly acquiescing to decisions they dislike. So there is greater commitment and energy for implementation. Finally, consensus decision making requires people to live out the values of mutual respect and consideration, while calling upon them to develop related skills for communication and process. And these benefits then carry over into other life arenas and activities.

On the downside, consensus can take more time than autocratic approaches, especially if people lack related experience and process skills. And it is usually inappropriate for crises and emergent situations which require immediate response and action, or for situations where participants lack maturity or competence.

What It Looks Like in Practice

So what does participatory governance and consensus decision making look like in practice? Social scientists have asked the same question and conducted extensive field research to answer it. Their early findings and a down-to-earth description were published decades ago and follow, along with a simplified flowchart of the process.

Participation in Practice

The elements of participation consist of: (1) group, rather than person-to-person, methods of supervision, (2) the open flow of information in all directions, and (3) the ability of all parties to exercise a measure of influence over outcomes.

A leader attempting to follow a participative pattern typically presents to his or her group a problem or task that faces them collectively. Before any decision has been made about it, the leader encourages everyone to share their view, makes his or her own view available without presenting it in such a way as to override others, and develops those processes that result in the pooling of all relevant information. From there the leader helps the group to develop an integrative solution to the problem at hand, one to which they are all willing to commit themselves.

In making decisions in this participatory fashion, there are facts—such as deadlines, financial constraints, and the like—which cannot be ignored if the organization is to achieve its objectives. It is the task of the leader to be fully aware of these situational requirements, and to make the group aware of them as well. In making decisions, the group should never lose sight of them.

The leader's responsibility is not to make the best decisions, but to structure and guide events so that the best decisions are made. Acquiring the knack of doing this is first and foremost a task of simply doing it, and learning by the doing.

Note: Excerpted and adapted from David Bowers, *Systems of Organization: Management of the Human Resource* (University of Michigan Press).

Process Flowchart for
Consensus Decision Making

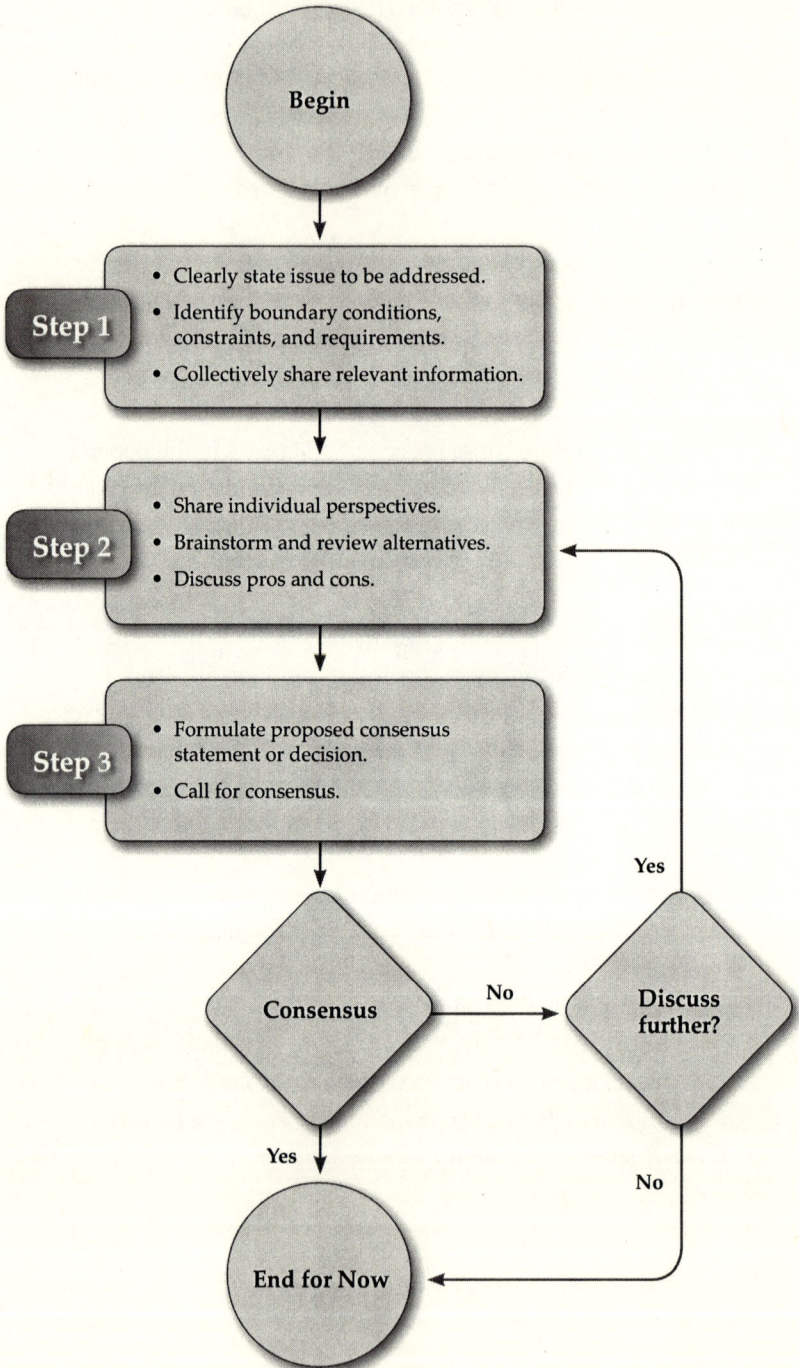

Begin

Step 1
- Clearly state issue to be addressed.
- Identify boundary conditions, constraints, and requirements.
- Collectively share relevant information.

Step 2
- Share individual perspectives.
- Brainstorm and review alternatives.
- Discuss pros and cons.

Step 3
- Formulate proposed consensus statement or decision.
- Call for consensus.

Consensus

No

Discuss further?

Yes

Yes

No

End for Now

II. The Council of Equals

Power can be likened to a candle.
If my candle is lit and I share the flame with those around me,
I have lost nothing; indeed I have gained because of
the increased light and warmth generated by multiple candles.

~Larraine Matusak

The Council of Equals _____

A *council of equals* is a group of people using consensus decision making to govern and manage an enterprise. Historical roots for it are found in myriad sources: indigenous cultures, classical Greece, ancient federations such as the Iroquois Confederacy, earth-based spiritual traditions, matriarchal societies, King Arthur's Round Table, Quaker meetings, and self-directed teams. So the spirit of council has appeared and reappeared across cultures and over the centuries, from ancient times to the present. It is a universal and timeless archetype of the human psyche, based upon the principles of human dignity, mutual respect, non-violence, and free will.

In a council of equals the focus is on the center, which holds the *governing ideas* of the enterprise. These compass headings include: (1) the purpose and mission statement, (2) a set of core values and beliefs, and (3) specific goals and strategies. This center is equidistant from and directly available to each member. The council's autonomy and authority are legitimate to the extent that the group stays on compass and abides by its governing ideas.

> **council of equals**
>
> a group of people
> using consensus decision making
> to govern and manage
> an enterprise

The council of equals is not a form of anarchy, nor does it do away with hierarchy. While a council holds and carries the collective power and authority of its individual members, its autonomy is limited and bounded by its governing ideas. In addition, a council is superseded by executive administration above it, if it is part of a larger organization, as well as by the legal statutes and regulatory codes of greater society.

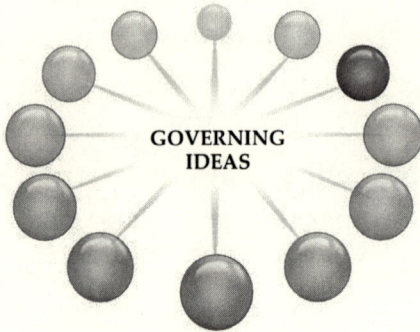

The First Among Equals

Most organizations require that a single individual—the designated leader or person in charge—be held accountable for a work group or team. Among other things, this person is expected and required to provide a reckoning for what does or does not happen. This arrangement entails a liability and risk for which the individual may be personally called to account. In a council of equals this person is referred to as the *first among equals*. Their place in the circle is designated by the darker sphere in the above schematic.

In this context, accountability is different from responsibility. While the first among equals is accountable for the group and overall outcomes, every member shares responsibility for getting the work done. In other words, each person is obligated to take action and make good faith effort in service to the governing ideas of the enterprise.

Historical roots for the term first among equals is most often traced back to the Roman Empire, where it was used for and by the Emperor as a way to reduce the appearance of dictatorship relative to the Senate. But more germane here is that the term was also used for the centurions in the early Roman army. These officers held rank over approximately 100 assigned citizen soldiers, but could not order any of them—free men—to do something. So they led by example: fighting at the foremost front of the line, displaying their courage and skills for the men behind to see. These centurions were thereby the ones *most at risk*, and they reportedly took heavy casualties.

> **first among equals**
>
> an individual held accountable for a group or team that operates solely on the basis of consensus decision making.

Since Roman times, variations of the concept have been applied in different political systems and religious institutions to indicate less autocracy than a dictatorship. The office of Prime Minister in the parliamentary system of Great Britain is one example, the word *prime* being derived from the Latin for first among equals—primus inter pares. Other applications of the concept include: the Chief Justice of the United States Supreme Court, the President of the European Commission, the Dean of the College of Cardinals of the Roman Catholic Church, the Ecumenical Patriarch of the Eastern Orthodox Church, and the Archbishop of Canterbury of the Anglican Communion.

It is worth noting that no decision can be made by the council without the support and endorsement of the first among equals. Of course, that applies to each of the other members as well. It is noted here because formal leaders are usually reluctant to use a council approach because they believe they will lose control of the group and its decision making. But that is not the case. What they lose is the ability to unilaterally impose their will on the group. Through their blocking rights, they still retain control to stop any decision they believe is grossly wrong and/or contradicts the governing ideas of the enterprise.

Term	Meaning
first	*Being Accountable.* Being responsible and liable for what does or does not happen; being expected to provide a reckoning on outcomes, and being personally at risk for such.
among	*Being in Community.* Governing and managing *with* others rather than *over* others; sharing power, authority, responsibility, information, rewards, and sacrifices.
equals	*Being a Peer.* Having the same amount of formal decision-making power as each of the other members in the group; not being able to unilaterally override them.

While accountability is the primary factor in designating a first among equals, such individuals are often distinguished in other ways within the group. As "the person in charge," they typically control extra resources, are networked with others who hold organizational power, have access to privileged information, are familiar with key issues, and have special training or knowledge.

While organizations usually establish single-person accountability for a group or a team, there can be more than one first among equals on a council. Such shared accountability may also occur in autocratic systems. For example: the executive officers for a board of trustees share legal accountability in cases of malfeasance or wrongdoing; married couples are held jointly accountable in society for raising their children; and business partners share financial accountability (profit versus loss) for their enterprise. Similarly, informal venues often have no single person designated as the first among equals. In these cases, accountability is shared by and distributed throughout the group.

Chain of Command

Council members are mutually accountable to one another for their contributions, behavior, and performance. They therefore report to the council as a whole, rather than to a single individual. Thus, the *chain of command* for a council goes from the individual member → to the council as a whole → to higher level administration within the organization (if applicable) → and lastly, to regulatory and governmental agencies outside the organization.

Decisions made by the council or a council member can be appealed by notifying and meeting directly with the council. Rather than approach the entire council, parties may elect to approach an individual council member of their choice. That member is then responsible for bringing the issue forward to the council as a whole. If the appeal is unsuccessful at the council level, parties may then carry their appeal forward to higher administrative authority, first inside and then outside the organization.

Because the performance and behavior of any individual on the council is the business of the entire council, concerns relating to a particular member are addressed by the group with that individual. That applies to performance reviews, merit increases, and salary issues, as well as any discipline. The only exception is the first among equals, who formally reports jointly to the council and a higher-level executive or governing body (if the group is part of a larger organization). When an issue concerns an individual member in terms of performance or discipline, then he or she loses their decision-making power at the table. The member may still take part in the process and offer contributions, but because of the conflict of interest the individual is not included in the related decision making.

In general, the group stands as a whole rather than as individuals. As long as a member's intentions are judged to be upright, discipline is not used to address performance problems or other issues. Individuals working in good faith can count on the continued support of the other members. Individual performance issues, therefore, are usually handled by self-correction and/or compensating actions by the other council members.

Congruency and Authenticity

The council framework offers some unique challenges for a leadership group, specifically: How can the group maintain its strength of diversity in member perspectives and avoid groupthink, while sustaining itself as an integrated and effective team? And how can council members be authentic as individuals and still congruent as a leadership body? The following chart is offered in response.

from Many Minds...to One Voice

Phase I

Many Minds and Many Voices

Each council member begins the decision-making process with a unique and valuable perspective to share. These "many minds" and "many voices" are critical assets of the group that need to be appreciated, nurtured, and affirmed.

Phase II

Group Process and Consensus

After sharing their perspectives, the council proceeds through a process that concludes with a consensus decision. That decision is deemed to be the best joint resolution or action among the alternatives for the group given the parameters of:

(1) the range and depth of support for the option within the council,

(2) the limited time and resources available to address the issue,

(3) what is achievable within the context of present realities, and

(4) congruency with the council's governing ideas.

Phase III

Shared Understanding and One Voice

Each council member understands the unique perspectives of the other members, and why the council reached the decision or position that it did. They can, therefore, each speak in a common voice on behalf of the council in sharing such.

III. Making It Work

Experience is the mother of all learning

~Will and Ariel Durant

Good Faith

The power granted to council members is based upon principles of right intention and action. These are binding upon each member and serve to promote what is necessary for the council to: (1) be a legitimate governing body, and (2) function effectively as a team. In a nutshell, it is incumbent upon council members to use their stations to achieve the organization's collective purpose. This commitment and obligation are crucial to participatory governance, assuring that the shared power and authority are used primarily to further the mission of the enterprise, rather than personal ambitions and self-interest.

Thus, council members need to engage in good faith. This *good faith* is defined as having and demonstrating a sincere commitment to serve the collective purpose and governing ideas of the enterprise. It encompasses working with good intentions, trust, honesty, and motivation beyond self-interest to accomplish the group's mission and goals.

good faith

1. having and demonstrating a genuine intention and sincere commitment to serve the collective purpose and governing ideas of the enterprise

2. working with good intentions, trust, honesty, and motivation beyond self-interest to accomplish the group's mission and goals

Good faith is the glue that holds a council together. It generates the trust needed for authenticity and connection, while creating a safe container and space in which people can comfortably take risks and be creative. Without good faith and trust, the council framework will not work. Each member of the council shares responsibility for nurturing and safeguarding these core assets and social goods.

Good faith entails—first and foremost—a genuine intention to serve the collective purpose and governing ideas of the enterprise. Actions and behavior flow from there. From this perspective, intentions are primary and behavior is secondary. After all, unwise or hurtful actions can sometimes occur even with the best of intentions. So what does good faith look like in practice? Indicators include:

- being sincere, open, honest, and trustworthy
- keeping commitments
- being appreciative and supportive of other members
- demonstrating trust in the group process
- assuming a perspective that embraces what is best for the enterprise
- serving as a responsible steward for designated areas of responsibility
- holding yourself and others accountable

Even though we can identify such indicators, it is really not possible to codify good faith in terms of a comprehensive listing of specific do's and don'ts. That's because there are infinite possibilities and expressions for human action, compounded by the uniqueness of particular situations and different contexts. Our myriad laws and regulatory codes, growing daily to address the latest innovations and trends in wrongdoing, bear testimony to that. The council approach therefore depends more upon our basic sense of recognition and knowingness—that is, we know good faith when we see it—rather than upon a prescribed list of coded behavior.

Individuals who are unwilling or unable to make a good faith commitment and so compass their behavior are unsuitable for council membership. Members who violate their good faith commitment, either grossly or chronically (repeatedly), need to be censured and removed from the council.

In making decisions on behalf of the enterprise, members are sometimes confronted with potential conflicts of interest. The good faith way for handling such is *disclosure*: openly declaring any special relationships or self-interest. This gives other members notice to pay attention, and permission to raise any questions or concerns. In extreme cases, a council member may believe that he or she is personally unable to make an unbiased decision and/or that it would be in the best interest of the organization for someone else to make a particular decision. In such cases, the conflicted member is expected to take the initiative to involve others or withdraw from the decision-making process.

Documentation

To clarify member understanding and commitment to the enterprise, it is immensely helpful to craft written documents on the following:

1. *The Governing Ideas.* These include the purpose and mission statement, values and beliefs, and major goals of the enterprise.

2. *A Group Charter.* This is a good faith statement signed by each of the council members, committing to serve the organization's collective purpose and governing ideas.

If the council is part of a larger organization, these documents need to be authorized and countersigned by a higher-level executive or group. Rather than being just paper artifacts, they are touchstones and compass headings for the council—powerful resources for those inevitable moments when the group is scratching its collective head, trying to reappraise things or get its bearings while addressing a difficult issue.

Meetings and Gatherings

Meetings and gatherings are where a council comes together to get its group work done: namely, doing and accomplishing the management functions described earlier. And the closer the group is to the action, the more often it needs to meet. For example, a self-directed team on a factory floor may meet daily at the start of their work shift, whereas a board of trustees for a small non-profit may meet only quarterly. This can be done face-to-face or virtually, via conference calls and such. However the connections are made, it is vitally important that any meeting or gathering be an effective and personally worthwhile experience for coucil members.

The content and structure for these get togethers consist of: (1) the topics to be addressed, (2) the specific objectives desired in addressing each topic, and (3) the particular activities or processes used to accomplish those objectives. The designated time together is then divided or segmented by topic.

When we think of meetings we usually picture people sitting around a table and either discussing things or listening to a presentation or report. However, a group can engage in a wider variety of ways, such as: brainstorming a list of alternatives, doing individual writing, role playing, categorizing items, or breaking into subgroups. These and other types of activities can bring life and energy to meetings and gatherings, stimulating productivity and creativity while fostering a sense of satisfaction and worthwhile engagement. The point is: the specific activity used by the group ought to depend upon the purpose and goals in addressing the particular topic. And goals for a specific topic at a particular get together will vary, including one or more of the following:

- share information
- obtain input (get feedback, suggestions, or information from the group)
- advance the thinking on an issue (e.g., analyze a problem, identify root causes, define resolution criteria, evaluate options, edit a statement)
- make a decision
- improve communication
- build capacity (training and development)

Many council exchanges are relatively informal and require little process, such as sharing updates and announcements. So a council will spend a fair amount of time dealing with topics that require a simple decision or no decision at all. But some topics can be particularly challenging, requiring that the group solve a complex problem or make a major decision about a controversial policy. These topics and exchanges require more formality and processing, and sometimes a dedicated get together outside the normal meeting venues.

Regular Meetings

The following template and protocols are recommended for regular meetings: (1) start the meeting, (2) handle the easy items and quick business, (3) address the major and substantive items, (4) take a break, (5) address other substantive items, (6) evaluate and end the meeting. With time and experience, the protocols can be normalized and integrated by the group, eventually becoming a natural way of being and doing together instead of an organized process and recipe. Generally, the group needs to be more rather than less formal when one or more of the following conditions apply:

- the group or some of its members lack experience in working together as a council of equals
- relatively little time is scheduled and available for addressing the items on the agenda
- one or more of the issues on the agenda is complex, difficult, or controversial

Regardless of the level of formality, every meeting requires an agenda, which is a game plan for the get together. A preliminary one for the next meeting should be drafted

MAKING IT WORK | 47

at the end of the preceding one and included in the minutes. This provides members time to reflect upon and prepare for related discussions and decision making (while keeping an open mind for the group process ahead). The agenda can then be revised and finalized at the beginning of the meeting itself.

1st **Order of Business** **Open Meeting**

Attendees conduct a check-in round by succinctly responding to the question: "What's most on my mind right now?" or "What does it feel like to be me today?" This helps people to temporarily set aside whatever else is going on in their lives and be present for the meeting ahead. It also helps them to connect with one another beyond their roles in the group. However, it is important that no one respond to what is shared, at least not during the meeting itself. And if anyone prefers not to share, which is perfectly OK, they can simply say, "I'm in."

2nd **Order of Business** **Fill Key Roles**

There are key roles that need to be accomplished during a meeting: facilitator, timekeeper, and minute taker. The facilitator has the lion's share of responsibilities:

- open the meeting
- finalize the agenda
- keep the meeting on track, per the agenda
- assure that everyone is heard

- clarify all outcomes and decisions in straightforward language
- close the meeting

The timekeeper tracks the elapsed time spent on specific issues and the meeting in general, alerting the group as needed to keep things on schedule. The minute taker takes notes during the meeting to record the activities and decisions.

These responsibilities can be divided up differently. However that is done, the goal is to distribute the work of managing the meeting among different members so that each member is able to participate as a peer. With that in mind, there are significant advantages to regularly rotating these roles among the group. First, doing so increases the group's depth in fulfilling them, so that absences of particular members do not overly impact functioning the group. Second, by the different members learning how to fulfill each role, the related functions become instilled and embedded throughout the group. After a while, the formally assigned roles of facilitator and time keeper can fall away as each member is naturally doing them.

3rd Order of Business Finalize Agenda

Beginning with the preliminary agenda, the group brainstorms and lists whatever else needs to be addressed. Once the list is pared down and finalized, the group can review the order. If the meeting is expected to be easy or routine, the agenda items can be left in the random order they were identified and written down. However, if the meeting might be difficult, ordering the items in a strategic way can be very helpful. To do that, place information sharing and housekeeping type items at the beginning of the agenda. Schedule important or difficult items in the middle, with a specified outcome and a reasonable allotted time for each. Place remaining items that are not urgent towards the end of the meeting, so that if the group runs out of time the topics of immediate importance will have been covered. Once the agenda is finalized, it should be posted. That way everyone can see where the group is during the meeting and how much remains to be done within the time available.

Some topics or items may need to span several meetings. To handle these, first identify the overall end result for the endeavor and then the limited specific goals for each meeting. That way, needed progress can be made on large scale undertakings while still leaving room for other items to be addressed.

4ᵗʰ Order of Business   Conduct Meeting

Proceed through the agenda. For items that require processing and a decision, the group:

1. shares the relevant information at hand
2. reviews any constraints and requirements
3. shares perspectives with an eye toward the governing ideas and reaching a decision
4. develops and reviews options

5. makes a consensus-based decision, and then
6. identifies any related action items (who, what and when?)

These steps are repeated until all the items have been dealt with and the meeting is over.

For minor issues and items, the group can use a couple of modified approaches to reach consensus. One approach is based on the principal of *no objection*, whereby decisions are made when no objections are raised. Members are simply asked: "Does anyone have objections to the proposed?" If none are raised, the proposal stands as a decision. The other approach is to handle some issues by a majority vote. These short-cuts can be taken if the issue is a minor one and there is a consensus to take a vote on it. Their purpose is a practical one: to provide more time to address issues that really matter.

5th **Order of Business** **Close Meeting**

It is critically important for the council to have integrity and keep its commitments, which includes the seemingly mundane, like starting and ending meetings on schedule. Members need to be able to count on that when making other arrangements and commitments in their lives. Meetings, therefore, should never run over their allotted time unless the group consensually renegotiates this during the meeting itself. For longer meetings, a short mid-point break of five to ten minutes helps keep people fresh and creative. However, even with a break, experience has shown that *The Law of Diminishing Returns* begins taking an increasingly heavy toll after two hours of meeting time.

The check-out round consists of members responding in a concise manner to the following: "How did the meeting go? Specifically: What went well? And what needs to be improved upon?" After that they check-out by saying, "I'm out." Here again, it is important not to respond to what is shared.

6th Order of Business — Issue Minutes

Notes of the meeting need to be written and distributed promptly. For this and other reasons, the minute taker should craft and read what will be in the minutes during the meeting itself. This can be done by sharing a proposed summary statement after handling each agenda item, getting general agreement on it. Minutes are then approved as they are being drafted, and everyone is clear on what has been agreed upon. But they are not transcripts: they are a succinct summary of what was covered and needs to be remembered. So they generally need to include:

- announcements
- a list of any handouts
- a summary statement for each topic discussed and the status
- clear statements of any decisions reached
- agreed-upon action items and related follow-up assignments

- outstanding action items and carry-overs from previous meetings
- upcoming events
- preliminary agenda for next meeting
- date, time, and place of next meeting

Guests and Visitors

Council meetings should be as open as possible to promote transparency and enable interested parties to connect directly with the council. Guests should be welcome, but required to contact a council member beforehand for permission to attend. Non-members might attend a council meeting to:

- appeal a decision made by the council or a council member
- share information, expertise, or concerns with the council
- serve as a representative or ambassador on behalf of others
- present a proposal
- observe the council at work

Most often, guests want to meet with the council because they have some sort of business to conduct with it. If that is the case, the item should be placed early on the agenda, so that the individual can be excused afterward and avoid having to sit through what is not important or relevant to them. But being a guest or visitor is not the same as having a place at the table. The council therefore needs to be clear about what level of engagement the guest is allowed, and assure that he or she is aware of such beforehand.

While transparency is to be valued and nurtured, portions of council meetings may nevertheless need to be closed to maintain confidentiality. Some groups consider their check-in process to be protected time and arrange for any guests to enter the circle afterward. Other issues or topics that might warrant protected time include:

- conversations related to difficult and controversial issues
- individual performance reviews or discipline
- proprietary information about products or services
- topics and issues connected with union contracts during labor negotiations
- anything so designated by a higher administrative authority

If guests are attending the meeting for other business, confidential items should be placed later in the meeting so that the guests can be excused beforehand.

Absent Members

Absent members may have an important contribution to make on some topics or be personally invested in a particular issue. In those instances, any decision should be tentative or conditional until they, too, consent to it.

Periodic Gatherings

Periodic gatherings are usually needed in addition to regular meetings. These provide longer stretches of contact time for the group to: (1) develop its capacities, and (2) keep the enterprise free and clear of clutter and unresolved issues. In the spirit of council, such gatherings need to be based upon collaboration and co-creation: planned and designed by those involved. Content for these in-depth sessions can include:

- having dialogues on especially difficult issues
- doing strategic planning
- conducting performance assessments
- organizing major new initiatives
- reviewing and improving the effectiveness of regular meetings
- conducting training and development sessions
- creating and revising administrative infrastructure

Due to the nature of the content, it can be very helpful to use outside facilitators (to help with group process), consultants (to give advice), and/or trainers (to teach skills). See *Appendix A* for resources and expertise on planning and facilitating such gatherings.

These get togethers can be enhanced significantly via off-site locations, overnight experiences, and/or potluck meals. Off-site locations help people to break out of habitually restrictive patterns of interaction. Overnights foster the same while also providing members more opportunities for getting to know one another better. And of course, potlucks are a wonderful way to share and connect. All of these formats can facilitate a deeper movement into relationship and authenticity, high-leverage qualities of an effective council.

Unfortunately, groups usually overlook these vitally important but not urgent gatherings. With the press of other matters in our busy lives, it is easy to forego them, especially when things seem to be going OK. But doing so is false economy: the time saved is more than offset by the troubles that naturally accrue and beset any group of people working closely together that does not proactively engage in these ways.

More about Consensus and Blocking

With consensus, each member has the power to block a decision by the group. But blocking is not used to further a personal preference. Rather, it is reserved for when a member believes that the proposed decision or action is so seriously wrong that the group should not be allowed to proceed with it. In other words, the member believes that the decision violates the governing ideas of the enterprise—such as the mission statement or core values. As noted earlier, as long as a proposed decision is blocked the status quo prevails. Because of the extraordinary power granted to individuals via their blocking rights and the ramifications for the group in someone exercising such, it is crucial for members to be clear about it.

In addressing any situation or issue, several viable options are usually available to a group. Of course, some options are undoubtedly better than others. But due to individual differences—in experience, temperament styles, organizational roles, functional expertise, and myriad other factors—group members will naturally have different preferences for addressing almost any issue. For that reason, blocking is not used as a mechanism for forwarding a preference or option. Doing so would paralyze a council's decision-making process. Preferences, therefore, need to stand on their own legs rather than on the power of a block, moving forward and being adopted based on a compelling rightness sensed by the group. After all, the goal of the group is not to arrive at a perfect or ideal solution, but the best one for the group at this particular time—one that everyone can endorse and support. Thus, the challenge for council members is to be able to:

1. champion or represent a given preference or option, if moved to do so;
2. come to understand each of the options being forwarded by others; while
3. remaining open and able to creatively formulate new options through the group process; and ultimately,
4. discerning the best option that everyone will support.

Interestingly, that best option may be one person's first choice and another's last choice. Thus, members need to have the wherewithal to support options that are not their first preference but are congruent with the governing ideas. This is not to imply that someone's first choice will never be adopted by the group. Indeed, that is usually the case. And oftentimes that option is the preferred first choice for everyone. But when the group lacks unanimity on the preferred first choice, it needs to have the capacity to discern the common ground that everyone can support in order to make a decision and move forward together.

On the other hand, while reaching consensus means that the group has common ground for going forward together, it does not necessarily indicate the level of commitment and quality of the energy members might have for the endeavor. Support can range from enthusiastic ("I really like it!") to lukewarm ("I can live with it.") to neutral ("It doesn't affect me."). For certain issues then, it may be important to check out the level of commitment and energy that group members have for the decision and implementation, particularly if the stakes are high and one or more of the following factors apply:

- the issue is critically important or controversial
- the decision will have a long-term impact
- implementation requires significant resources
- the decision is irreversible
- implementation depends on significant autonomous action of the members downstream

Nevertheless, if someone truly believes that a proposed decision violates the governing ideas of the enterprise, he or she is duty-bound to block the decision and thereby prevent the group from adopting it. In those cases—which are rare—the individual is quite possibly providing the requisite leadership for safeguarding both the legitimacy of the council as a governing body and the well-being of the enterprise. Faced with a block, the council must decide what to do next.

Sometimes not reaching a decision or consensus might not be an option. This most often occurs in cases where the council is superseded by a higher administrative authority, such as an executive directive in the larger organization or promulgation by an external regulatory agency. Failure to comply would be tantamount to insubordination (in the former) or breaking the law (in the latter). Such issues can be time-bound, requiring a non-status quo response and/ or immediate action. To handle these, some groups have adopted a *Time is of the Essence Rule,* which allows them to shift from consensus decision making to a majority vote. But this is not recommended unless the matter is relatively unimportant. It is far better for a council to hold its feet to the fire: staying in process until it reaches a consensus on how to proceed or respond.

Dialogue

While there are myriad ways for a council to work on something, there are two basic ways for a council to talk about something: *discussion* and *dialogue.* And they are very different in terms of both process and outcomes.

Discussion versus Dialogue

Discussion is used to arrive at a singular point of view quickly, so that a group can make a decision and take action. It emphasizes individual perspectives: people focus on sharing their opinions and trying to convince others to see things a certain way. As a result, they tend to talk past one another. Nevertheless, discussion is very useful for addressing issues that are minor or clear-cut, and/or when there isn't time available for more processing.

It is worth noting that the word *discussion* has the same Latin root as *concussion* and *percussion—cussio*, which means "to shake violently." While discussions are intended for sharing perspectives in a civil manner, they often go awry when dealing with difficult or complex issues, leaving people *shaken* mentally, emotionally and socially. Difficulties arise because we tend to identify with our opinions and points of view, albeit unconsciously. And when that happens, a critique of our position can feel personal. Other positions—and sometimes even those putting forward such—can then be viewed as problems or threats that need to be addressed and overcome. This pitfall can be avoided through the practice of dialogue.

Dialogue is used by a group to think out loud together. The process emphasizes collective understanding and synthesis, rather than winning others over to a particular point of view. Through dialogue, insights and wisdom can emerge that illuminate new possibilities for consensual action. It is therefore invaluable for addressing issues that are complex,

> ### dialogue
>
> the act of thinking out loud together
>
> a conversation with a center, but no sides

controversial and/or important. But dialogue takes time, sometimes an hour or more for processing a single issue.

More about Dialogue

Used by indigenous people, the early Greeks and others, dialogue is a form of group inquiry into the thinking that underlies individual opinions and positions. The word *dialogue* comes from the Greek roots *dia* for "through" and *logos* for "meaning." And it is generally understood to be a conversation of mutual discovery into how we think about things. Experientially, however, it is much more than that: it is a conversation in which the human spirit is evoked and present.

In dialogue, we do not have to have things figured out beforehand. In fact, it helps to have an unmade-up mind. That is not to say that some prior thinking should not be done about an issue, but that our thinking needs to remain open for the upcoming conversation. So even though we may be predisposed to a particular position or opinion, we need to remain curious and interested about what others think and where the conversation will go. After all, each person—including our self—is carrying part of the truth. So we can wonder: "How is it that this other person sees things differently than I do? What part of the larger truth am I missing or overlooking here? And how does the truth he or she is carrying relate to the truth I am carrying?" With experience, we come to trust the larger knowingness and capacity of the group, while still respecting how we see things ourselves.

The "How To" of Dialogue

Imagine a group of people coming together to make a soup or stew, each person showing up with different ingredients that they toss into a large kettle on a woodstove in the center of the room. Standing around and stirring the conglomeration, people take turns putting things in, sampling it, and making adjustments until there is a general agreement that it is cooked and ready. Dialogue is like that. But instead of a kettle on a stove there's just space in the middle of the room. And instead of vegetables and spices, we throw in thoughts, feelings, opinions, assumptions, conclusions, rationale, perspectives, and questions.

In dialogue we talk to the center, rather than directly to one another. This practice helps to avoid discussion and to separate positions from personal identities. Think of it as a conversation with a center, but no sides. Once something is shared and lands in the center, it becomes community property. In this way the group holds all of what is being offered and investigated, thereby developing a shared understanding on the issue. It is not that everyone thinks the same way or agrees on a particular perspective, but that the group develops a shared knowing and understanding of each of the different perspectives. This enables members to hold and consider complex and difficult issues from different points of view without getting personally entangled in them. The result is a free exploration that brings to the surface the full range and depth of people's experience and thinking, while enabling them to move beyond individual perspectives in powerful ways.

Because discussion is the norm in our society, people usually need some help and structure in learning how to do dialogue. The following basic steps and guidelines are therefore suggested.

Step 1   **Build the Container**

The first step for having a dialogue is to build a safe container for the conversation—a space and atmosphere where people can feel comfortable to show up without fear of retribution. This is accomplished by:

Seating and Introductions. Seat participants in a circle, so that they can easily see one another without straining. Introduce any guests and clarify how they are connected to the issue at hand. Ask people to turn off their cell phones.

Check-ins. Do a quick check-in round, as explained previously in the section on *Regular Meetings*.

Confidentiality Agreement. Post and read aloud the following confidentiality agreement: "Sharing generalities afterward with others is OK. Sharing 'who said what' is not OK." Do another round, asking each participant to verbally agree to this by saying either, "I agree," or "No, I don't agree." Excuse anyone who chooses not to make the commitment.

| Step 2 | **Review the Basics** |

Once the container is set, review the following definitions and guidelines. Write and post them for everyone to clearly see and refer to.

Dialogue. The art and practice of thinking out loud together. A conversation with a center, but no sides.

Purpose of Dialogue. To share perspectives about a specific topic or issue, rather than defend a given position.

Goal of Dialogue. To create shared understanding in the group, rather than make a decision. This understanding includes knowing each of the perspectives of the other participants, along with the underlying assumptions and rationale.

Guidelines for Participants

√ Relax…Let go of the need to resolve anything.
√ Make a conscious intention and genuine effort to understand others.
√ Slow down…Create silent space (3 breaths) between speakers.
√ Prior to speaking, acknowledge the last person who spoke.
√ Speak from the "I" position.
√ Speak to the center rather than to another person.
√ Be concise…Say only what is essential and needs to be said.
√ Monitor and manage yourself accordingly.

| Step 3 | **Conduct the Dialogue** |

Having the dialogue is next. To get started, someone offers a question to the center of the circle that is related to the issue at hand. That question needs to be open-ended but crystal clear on what the particular issue is. Then after two or three minutes of timed silence, participants are free to begin speaking per the guidelines. Some groups find it helpful to use a *talking stick*. Only the person with the artifact is able to speak. And for groups new to dialogue, it is very helpful to stop every fifteen minutes or so to check on how well the guidelines are being followed. In this way, the group can get periodic feedback and self-correct as needed.

Someone needs to serve as timekeeper, and notify the group a short time before the scheduled end of the session. At that point, the group can choose to renegotiate the allotted time or continue as scheduled. It is also recommended to reserve enough time at the end of a dialogue to go around the circle with the question: "Is there anything else that has *not* been said that you would like to share?" This question helps draw out perspectives and wisdom that were not shared during the conversation.

Step 4   Disassemble the Container and Check Out

The last step entails disassembling the container via a check-out process, which consists of a simple round in which each person says, "I'm out."

To facilitate reaching consensus on very difficult or seemingly intractable issues, it helps to postpone any decision making immediately after a dialogue. While this is not always possible, there are some significant advantages to doing such. First, knowing that a decision is not imminent helps people to let go and really listen during the conversation itself. Second, the downstream mental soak time can be very helpful. After all, it is difficult for most of us to turn on a dime when it comes to changing our mind, and a good night's sleep can do wonders in being influenced by our experience. New insights can arise related to the common ground we have with others, and to how seemingly contradictory perspectives can actually fit into a larger view of things. These can lead to formulating new and creative alternatives for the group.

Early attempts at dialogue usually feel clunky or unnatural, but that quickly dissipates with a little experience. With even more experience, the props for definitions and guidelines are no longer needed. And over time, a group will build capacity to naturally move into and out of dialogue, depending on the circumstances and context.

The dialogue experience evokes a sense of lightness. Feeling understood by others leads to an easing and fluidity in both our sense of being and in our perspective. We learn that we are not our positions—that we can put them on and take them off like clothes. We can better see the bigger picture and how seemingly contradictory things fit together. And most importantly, we discover through direct personal experience that the group does indeed have the wherewithal to address difficult and complex issues, figuring things out and moving forward together.

The egalitarian nature of the council framework helps participants to show up and be authentic in dialogue. This personal presence is what Native American traditions call *original medicine*: a unique beingness found nowhere else on the planet and therefore a potentially valuable resource for the community. It is also a bridge of connection and relationship to others, as well as a doorway into the ineffable world of the human spirit. All of this leads to greater understanding, better decision making and more innovative action, along with a greater sense of ease, joy, and fun. New and wonderful things become possible.

Dialogue is learned by simply doing it. The best way is for an experienced facilitator to lead a group through some relevant—and ideally difficult—conversations interspersed with some feedback and theory. Indeed, real-world challenging issues are the best raw material for learning dialogue. Just a few sessions can get a group up and running.

Skills for Dialogue

Listen	Be still…Consciously receive whatever is being shared and is coming in.
Abide	Witness your thoughts, feelings, emotions, body sensations, associations, and memories as they arise. Simply be aware of them, and then let them go…Don't rehearse what you are going to say. Focus instead on understanding what others are saying, and trust that you will say what is needed when the time comes.
Inquire	Ask questions that promote understanding.
Reflect	Slow the conversation down…Create spaces of silence between contributions to provide time to take in and reflect upon what was said.

Delegation and Interventions

Although it is important for a council to have enough meaningful material to work on together, it is also important to keep in mind that in most cases not everyone can do or be directly involved in everything. Otherwise, the council venues will be choked with minutia and busyness. The group therefore needs to develop a knack for the art of delegating within itself, whereby individual members and subgroups can do much of the needed work outside of meetings and gatherings.

As much as possible, the council needs to share its power and freedom with those engaged on its behalf and working under its auspices, resisting the pull or temptation to control and micromanage what it entrusts to others. On occasion, however, it may be necessary for the council to intervene with particular individuals or assigned subgroups. It has legitimate authority to do so when one or more of the following conditions apply:

- the council is requested to intervene by the affected individual or subgroup itself

- the council perceives that an individual or subgroup may lack the competency or ability to handle a critical problem or responsibility

- the council has reason to believe that the governing ideas or good faith commitment may have been violated

- the council is directed to intervene by a higher administrative authority

Interventions may consist of follow-up by a single member assigned by the council, by an appointed subgroup, or by the entire council.

Linkage

A council needs to effectively link itself with others, particularly those it serves, depends upon, and/or is interdependent with. To that end, it is helpful to have designated members of the council serve as *linkpins* for connecting with others. This linkage entails a continuous process of monitoring and exchange to promote mutuality and synergy. For this to work, members serving as linkpins need to: (1) function as clear and open channels of communication between the connecting individuals and groups, and (2) be able to influence the council on behalf of their contacts and vice versa, delivering support to and from the council in ways that meet the legitimate needs of both the council and those linked. Other mechanisms for linkage includes subgroups, task forces, ad hoc and informal discussions and dialogues, friendships, mentorships, workshops, and retreats.

Training and Development

Council members need to have the following mix of complementary capacities in order to accomplish their work together:

- technical and functional expertise
- problem-solving and decision-making skills
- interpersonal skills related to group process

The first category—technical and functional expertise—will vary with the particular enterprise and its field of endeavor (e.g., business, education, government, health care). Given the range and depth of some organizations, it is not unusual for a council to have a variety of functional specialists in the group. In such cases, the group often defers or gives extra weight to such individuals in deciding what to do about an issue related to their particular field of expertise.

However, the other categories—problem-solving, decision-making, and interpersonal skills related to group process—are generic and applicable to any field of endeavor or enterprise. It is worthwhile for members to learn more about these critical skills via available resources, materials and training. Several are listed in *Appendix A*. Nevertheless, as one historian put it: "Experience is the mother of all learning." So regardless of whether or not any formal training is done, the fact is: Dealing with the matters at hand are not merely occasions to get work done, but they are also important opportunities for personal learning and group development.

Confidentiality

The nature of council is non-secretive, so as much as possible the system should be an open book. Information on revenue, income, expenses, costs, individual performance, group performance, salaries, merit pay and other metrics or assessments should all be freely and readily available. Nevertheless, there are times when a council has legitimate grounds for confidentiality, including:

- while processing a difficult and controversial issue
- when necessary to protect proprietary information about products or services
- when addressing issues connected with union contracts during labor negotiations

- when directed to do so by a higher administrative
  authority

Of course, a council may choose other occasions and reasons to maintain confidentiality. But it needs to be done
consciously and clearly since the ability for members to
maintain cofidentiality plays a critical role in building and
sustaining the trust required for group effectiveness. All
of this becomes an important juggling act, balancing the
legitimate and seemingly competing needs between: (1)
openness and transparency, (2) care for individual members and the council itself, and (3) consideration for other
stakeholders and society. Nevertheless, experience dem-
onstrates that it is far more effective and worthwhile to
focus vital council energies on accepting and addressing
what is, rather than protecting and defending anything
through secrecy and obfuscation.

For a number of reasons — ranging from someone's simple
curiosity about participatory governance in general to a
stakeholder's legitimate need to know something in particular — members are often asked about the council and
its business. So questions will arise as to how to be open
and transparent while still honoring confidentiality on
behalf of the group. The following guidelines for members
are offered in response.

1. *Respond to legitimate needs for information.* If the
   person is a member of the greater organization
   or other stakeholder, share the general status of
   the council's ongoing deliberation or the decision
   reached. If the topic or issue has been designated

as confidential by the council, inform the person accordingly.

2. *Talk about topics not stories.* Feel free to talk about topics and issues that have been resolved in the council, but do not share stories about other members or identify any sources of comments.

3. *Focus on your own experience.* Feel free to share your own experience of the council, but not someone else's.

4. *Avoid over-processing issues between council sessions.* Be careful not to overwork important ongoing issues with other members outside of the meetings. While such processing can help you to gain clarity and insight, going too far may deprive the council of valuable energy and an important opportunity for working through the issue together as a group.

5. *Invite the curious to a council meeting.* If a non-member expresses a sustained or recurring interest in the council and how it works, get approval from the group to invite that person to attend and witness a council meeting. Avoid being a habitual source of council-related information for a non-member, unless the individual is a stakeholder and/or you are functioning on behalf of the council as a linkpin to connect with the person.

6. *Be forthright about managing confidentiality.* Be very clear in the council about designating any matter as confidential. Follow-up promptly in the council whenever you deem that confidentiality has been breached or broken.

7. *Encourage transparency.* Question the need for anything to be held confidentially. Assure that maintaining such is warranted to safeguard legitimate needs and/or promote the greater good.

Assessment

A council needs to periodically assess its outcomes and appraise how things are going. The feedback is then used to compass and redirect efforts to sustain or increase the effectiveness of the enterprise. And the larger the enterprise is, the greater the need for a systematic documented approach.

The most effective approaches are holistic and use multiple perspectives for input, including council members themselves, customers, suppliers, and other stakeholders. Referred to as *360-degree assessments*, their goal is to get an accurate picture of reality. That information is then used by the council to formulate a wide range of actionable endeavors, from developing goals for individual members to crafting a strategic plan for the enterprise. These holistic approaches entail assessing things externally and internally, looking both outside and inside the council.

1. *External Assessments.* The look outward is focused through the lens of the council's governing ideas, including the mission statement, purpose, goals and strategies. Since these are usually about achieving specific desired outcomes in a particular venture and field of endeavor, the assessment factors vary widely from group to group. In formal organizations, the metrics often include: comparisons to applicable standards and benchmarks (e.g., profit versus loss), inputs and feedback from various stakeholders (e.g., customer satisfaction surveys), and reviews or certifications by independent third parties (e.g., financial audits).

2. *Internal Assessments.* The look inward is focused on how well members and the group are performing the governance and management functions, both individually and together as a whole. This encompasses tangible and intangible aspects, including member expertise in an area of specialization (as in the former) and levels of trust (as in the latter). Unlike external factors, which vary with the enterprise, these internal factors are common to all council groups and endeavors.

In assessing both of these areas—external and internal—it is essential for the council to: (1) choose which metrics to use, (2) establish a system and process to get the necessary data on the metrics, (3) monitor and periodically report out on them, (4) re-compass and respond appropriately, and then (5) repeat the cycle. This can be done formally or informally, in a big periodic way or in a small continuous way, as a system or as a way of being.

There are some simple but powerful approaches for doing internal assessments that are worth considering. The first one requires a dedicated council gathering and employs the use of an assessment instrument. Members begin by splitting up and completing the instrument in private. The seclusion helps them to better disclose what they really feel and believe about themselves and others. They then reconvene as a group and share their responses. A sample instrument follows, which can easily be adapted or revised.

Another approach uses an *advisory committee* to provide periodic input and feedback as requested. Committee membership can include representatives from stakeholder groups, functional experts in your field of endeavor, consultants on group process, executives from higher level administration, and/or respected individuals who are willing to help.

A third approach uses a *witness council*. Here the council requests one or more individuals they respect to formally witness a regular meeting or special gathering. These individuals are asked to: (1) silently witness the proceedings, (2) focus on group dynamics rather than the content of the discussion, and then (3) provide feedback and comments that would be of service. These last two approaches can be combined, whereby an advisory committee or some of its representatives participate in a witness council.

Internal Assessment
(Page 1 of 3)

Respect

Respect is about appreciating and accepting ourselves and others for who we are and present ourselves to be.

Q1: What do I appreciate about myself?

Q2: Is there something about myself that I cannot accept?

Q3: What do I appreciate about the other members?

Q4: Is there something about the other members that I cannot accept?

Q5: What do other members appreciate about me?

Q6: Is there something about me that they cannot accept?

Internal Assessment

Trust

Trust is about believing in the sincerity and competence of others.

Sincerity is about saying what we mean and doing what we say.

.

Q7: Am I sincere?

Q8: Do I believe that the other members are sincere?

Competence is about having the requisite skills, knowledge, and ability to do what is needed, including:
1. technical and functional expertise
2. problem-solving and decision-making skills
3. interpersonal skills related to group process

Q9: Am I competent in each of these domains?

Q10: Do I believe the other members are competent in each of their domains?

Internal Assessment
(Page 3 of 3)

Freedom of Expression

Freedom of expression entails:
(1) being transparent and speaking openly,
(2) listening and giving space to others, and
(3) maintaining confidentiality.

Q11: Am I comfortable speaking freely and openly, without fear of retribution?

Q12: Are the other members comfortable?

Q13: Do I provide space in the conversation for others to feel fully expressed and understood?

Q14: Do the other members do likewise for me?

Q15: Do I maintain confidentiality on behalf of the group?

Q16: Do the other members do likewise?

Q17: Is there anything else that hasn't been identified or addressed that I need to disclose?

Attitudes and Perspectives _____

How we think about things has a lot to do with the reality we perceive. As one sage put it: "With our thinking we create the world." The following is therefore offered for keeping in mind throughout the council experience.

- One of the most basic choices we have as human beings is whether to live from fear or from love. For mature and competent people, a council of equals is what the choice of love looks like in governance.

- What happens to us in life is not as important as how we choose to respond to what happens to us.

- The best way to address almost any significant issue or concern is forthrightly and sincerely. And the best ground to stand on for doing that is being committed to balancing the legitimate needs of all the affected parties.

- Never let what you cannot do interfere with what you can do.

- Each of us carries some part of the truth and embodies what Native Americans call *original medicine,* a unique beingness found nowhere else on the planet.

- Even though our different truths appear to be in contradiction to each other, there is a larger truth that transcends but embraces all of them. This larger truth can be discerned through clear thinking, an open heart, and process wisdom.

- People are generally trustworthy—acting in good faith and doing the best they can with what they've got.

- People support what they help to create. And what they create doesn't have to be perfect, just better than any of the alternatives.

- An effective integration of diverse views, experience, and skills produces wise action and sustainable outcomes.

- The work of this moment—whatever is at hand and needs to be addressed—is not only an opportunity to further the governing ideas and goals of the enterprise, but also an opportunity to live out who we are and aspire to be. Everything we face is an opportunity to walk our path.

IV. Handling Road Bumps

When the going gets tough, the weird get crazy.

~Carl Christoff

Supportive Conditions

Several conditions support participatory governance and the use of consensus. If a group is having difficulties, it is worthwhile checking these out through the following inquiry.

Supportive Conditions Inquiry
(Page 1 of 3)

Unity of Purpose

The group has a basic core of agreement about the governing ideas of the enterprise, including its purpose and boundary conditions. This unifying base is recognized and accepted as a common starting place by all members.

Q1: Are the governing ideas clear?

Q2: Are they uncontested?

Equal Access to Power

Members have equality in the decision-making process. Except for the power of blocking, no single member or subgroup can overrule the others in the group.

Q3: Is the general level of power in the decision-making process equal among the members?

Supportive Conditions Inquiry
(Page 2 of 3)

Autonomy of the Group

The group has enough autonomy and latitude to provide it meaningful engagement and work.

Q4: Is the greater organizational environment and culture non-hostile (supportive or neutral) toward the framework and group?

Q5: Does the group have enough responsibility to have a meaningful sense of purpose?

Q6: Are there too many mandates or is there too much interference from higher administrative authorities to warrant group engagement?

Q7: Is there enough latitude for the group to have a legitimate sense of autonomy?

Balance in the Group

There is a sincere and sensitive effort to have all members participate and contribute, despite differences in personal qualities and attributes.

Q8: Do the more active members draw out the less active members, creating opportunities for them to contribute?

Q9: Do the less active members feel understood?

Supportive Conditions Inquiry
(Page 3 of 3)

Skills, Willingness and Time

Developing the skills and capacity for participatory governance requires that group members:
(1) cooperatively engage and trust each other,
(2) develop their skills of participation, facilitation and communication, and
(3) work to improve their process for governing and making decisions together.

Q10: Has the group explicitly clarified its norms and expectations for one another?

Q11: Are members willing to examine and share their attitudes toward each other?

Q12: Are members willing to discuss and improve their group process skills of participation, facilitation, and communication?

Q13: Are members willing and able to spend the necessary time together to do all of this?

Blocks and Impasses

Once in a while, a council may find itself at an impasse in handling an issue. This can occur for a variety of reasons—any one or more of which can apply in a given situation—including:

1. the issue is complex, difficult and/or controversial
2. the group has not dedicated the requisite time for effectively handling the issue
3. the group lacks the wherewithal for dealing with the issue

In the last case, when the group lacks the wherewithal for effectively processing the issue, the best approach is to get outside help. This can be done by using a trainer (to teach needed process skills), a facilitator (to help with the group process), and/or a consultant (to give advice to the group). Such cases are valuable opportunities for growth and development of the group.

In other cases when a specific proposal is blocked, consider adopting it on a temporary or trial basis, with a formal expiration date. That way, if approved, it could be field-tested for a designated period of time, after which a final decision would be made on whether to permanently adopt it or not. Or, if not done previously, consider having a group dialogue on the issue. And if possible, postpone any decision to give members time to digest and be influenced by what they have heard in the group.

Beyond dialogue, there are other approaches that can be used to foster movement and facilitate consensus. See *Appendix A* for resources that provide innovative tools and creative processes that can help. Of course, they all involve more time and energy. But for significant and/or important issues, it is well worth the time for a council to stay in process until it figures out how everyone can go forward together. The challenging group dynamic is more than just an occasion to solve the matter at hand: it is also a significant opportunity for personal learning and for developing the capacities of the council as a whole.

The most difficult and intractable scenarios can be addressed by using techniques that help separate individuals from their positions and see things from a larger perspective. The first technique—effective for processing two opposing positions—consists of marking off a physical arena in the middle of the room with two sides (picture a miniature tennis court), one side designated for each of the opposing positions. The council forms an outer ring around the arena, thereby creating a circle of witnesses. Members then take turns entering and leaving the arena, spending time on both sides justifying and defending the designated perspective. Only those in the arena are allowed to talk, and there may be one or more members on each side of the arena at any one time. Each person entering the arena articulates the position of whatever side he or she is physically located on, and then eventually rotates to the other side and represents that position. Sometime afterward, the individual moves back into the witness circle. This *fishbowl* technique enables each member to physically and energetically embody both of the opposing positions, while providing other members a unique vantage point as spectators from which to witness and hold the conversation.

A second technique—effective for processing issues from several perspectives—entails designating specific chairs or seating for each of the particular positions. Group members seat themselves and then complete a round in which they each articulate the position designated for the chair they are sitting in. After that, everyone rotates their seating and repeats the process. To match the number of chairs to the number of council members, more than one chair can be designated for a given position. Such techniques can help people to understand and experience the individual truth of different perspectives, thereby creating a shared understanding that can lead to dramatic breakthroughs in finding common ground and creative alternatives.

If one or more members are still blocking the decision, consider checking member attitudes by asking the group to reflect on the following questions:

> *Blocking Member*. Has the blocking member examined his or her motives closely? Is their refusal to consent based on a strong belief that the decision is grossly wrong; that he or she would be doing a great disservice by allowing the group to go forward with it?

> *Council as a Whole*. Does the group believe the blocking member is acting in good faith?

Any concerns regarding the good faith of the dissenting member need to be addressed in a forthright manner. If there are no such concerns, then the group can consider simply laying the issue aside for another time. Of course, this is not always possible, especially if a higher-level administrative authority is requiring action. But if it is, time can be a powerful ally. While we often have a sense that a decision needs to be made right away, in many cases that just isn't so. As one practitioner put it: "Somehow the world continues to go around the sun—day after day, year in year out—whether we make a decision or not."

Not making a decision is not necessarily a failure, nor should it be stigmatized. It simply means that the group needs to find more common ground in order to move beyond the status quo together.

Interpersonal Conflict

Council members are expected to deal effectively with any concerns, conflicts, or negative feelings they have regarding other group members. If the matter appears to be resulting in significant harm, it needs to be brought forward. While group conflicts related to functional issues generally require dialogue, interpersonal conflicts between individual members generally require one-on-one processing. In the latter case, related discussions occur first between the individuals, and then, if necessary, in the council. When confronted with such—as one of the individuals or as part of the council—members are obliged to make themselves available and deal forthrightly with any concerns. A protocol for handling interpersonal conflict follows.

Protocol for Handling Interpersonal Conflict
(Page 1 of 2)

Step 1

Get Clear

The concerned member gets clear on the issue, then determines whether or not it merits use of the requisite time and energy to address it. If so, he or she considers using a third party to assist in a "reality check," and/or goes through the structured inquiry process outlined in the *Assessment* section. After that, the member decides to either let go of the issue or process it by engaging the other member.

Step 2

Inform and Share

The concerned member meets personally with the other member to inform and share. If things get "hot" remember to:

1. Stop and pause. Take 60 seconds or more of silence.

2. Seek first to understand (including feelings, emotions, and thoughts) and then to be understood.

3. Focus on and speak from your own experience.

If the issue is not resolved by the get together, the members proceed to Step 3 or Step 4.

Step 3

Get Help (Optional)

The two members jointly select and use a third party to facilitate further discussions or serve as a witness to such. If things are still not resolved, they proceed to Step 4.

Protocol for Handling Interpersonal Conflict
(Page 2 of 2)

Step 4

Address the Concern in Council

The members take the issue to the council for processing. Council decides to do one or more of the following:

1. If not already done, require that contesting members go through Step 3.

2. Assign the issue to another council member or subgroup for follow-up and handling.

3. Serve as a witness council for the contesting members.

4. Decide upon and resolve the issue. (*Note*: Contesting members have no blocking rights on this decision.)

5. Direct the concerned member to let go of the issue or concern.

Step 5

Appeal the Outcome

If the group is part of a larger organization and the member is not satisfied with resolution at the council level, the issue can be appealed to the next higher level of executive administration. If not part of a larger organization, the member needs to accept the decision or resign from the council.

Violations of Good Faith

Violations of the good faith agreement undermine the legitimacy of the group as a governing body and erode trust. They thereby cause significant harm and need to be treated seriously. A recommended *Protocol for Reviewing Good Faith* is provided on the following pages.

In reviewing member behavior on issues of good faith, consideration is given to: (1) the level of conscious action, and (2) the amount of harm done. The former relates to the motives and mental processes that preceded the action; the latter relates to the losses and damages that occurred or could have occurred. An individual under such review is excluded from the related decision-making process, and may also be restricted access by the council to portions of the related discussions and dialogue. The forthrightness and cooperation demonstrated by the member in question throughout any such process is considered an indication of his or her good faith.

Major transgressions can warrant removal from the council and even expulsion from the organization. In such cases, the focus is placed on censuring the guilty member and repairing the harm done. With the wrongdoer no longer a member, repairing the harm becomes the council's responsibility. For lesser transgressions, the focus is on learning and healing. Here responsibility falls on the transgressor to initiate and take whatever actions are necessary to: (1) integrate the learning, and (2) repair the harm done. The council holds the member accountable to do this and provides support as needed.

Protocol for Reviewing Good Faith

Step 1

Determine whether the good faith agreement was violated and, if so, the amount of harm done.

Gather information. Use the *Intentionality and Forethought* chart on the following page to help clarify the nature of the thinking process and level of conscious choice related to the action. Identify the harm and damage that occurred or could have occurred.

Losses can be tangible or intangible, including increased costs, lost time from work, loss or deterioration of assets, lower staff morale, loss of trust, bad feelings, negative impacts upon relationships, and loss of credibility for the individual, council or organization. Tangible losses are estimated. Intangible losses, if not estimable, are at least identified.

Step 2

If the good faith agreement was violated, determine whether the action warrants the member's removal from the council or termination from the organization.

Termination is warranted when the action violates specific legal statutes and/or organizational standards for which the precedent and norm is termination. Loss of council governance membership is warranted for offenses that were intentional and caused, or could have caused, significant harm or loss. If governance privileges are revoked, the member is reassigned by the council as appropriate. Reassignment may result in adjustments to position and salary.

Step 3

If the good faith agreement was violated but does not warrant termination or removal from the council, member proceeds to repair the harm done.

The transgressor is responsible for: (1) recognizing and admitting the mistakes made, (2) identifying the related learnings, and (3) taking initiative to repair the harm done. Council holds the member accountable for this and supports him or her as needed.

Degree of Intentionality and Forethought

Premeditated Action
Action involved conscious choice. Member had forethought and deliberately planned it.

☐ Member knew beforehand that it was wrong.

☐ Member disregarded potential harm to organization or others.

Conscious Action
Some level of mind was at work. It was a conscious choice of action.

☐ Member knew it was wrong but did it anyway.

☐ Action was repeated and/or had previously been identified as inappropriate.

Unmindful Action
Action was spontaneous and/or conditioned.

☐ Member performed action with no mental process or reflection about potential harm or damage.

☐ Action was a one-time event, out of character with the member's normal behavior.

Difficult Individuals

Sometimes—though rarely—a single individual is consistently at odds with everyone else in the group. In such cases, both the council and the individual need to consider whether this person is in the right organization or group. Most importantly, chronically difficult members need to be dealt with forthrightly. Related questions include:

1. Is the individual engaged in good faith?

2. Is he or she unreservedly committed to the governing ideas of the enterprise?
3. If so, is their psychological house in order?
4. And if it is, does the person have the requisite intention and skills for working in a participatory way with others?

V. Getting Started

The aim of life can only be
to increase the sum of freedom and responsibility
to be found in every person and the world.

~ Albert Camus

Preparation and Readiness _____

It is not necessary to fix everything prior to forming a council of equals. Nor is it necessary to have the requisite skills in problem-solving, conflict management, and group process. These can be developed experientially as the group deals forthrightly with its regular business and the matters at hand. Nevertheless, members need to be:

☑ competent in their functional areas of expertise

☑ committed to working in good faith on behalf of the enterprise and its governing ideas

☑ committed to accepting and supporting one another personally and professionally

☑ willing to hold one another accountable and candidly address any issues

Staging into the Model _____

It is possible for a group to stage into the model over time—say a year or two, gradually taking on increasing range and levels of responsibility. This staging is basically a matter of systematically expanding participation in the management functions. Sample phases may include:

Phase 1   work and vacation scheduling

Phase II   quality assurance and work process improvement

Phase III budgeting and financial control

Phase IV staffing (hiring, training, assessment and discipline)

Phase V strategic planning

Phasing can be designed and tailored for the particular group and its context. The group simply begins training and working in a consensual manner in Phase I, then progressively moves through the subsequent phases until it is eventually accomplishing all the management functions together on a consensus basis.

Start-up

Specific milestones for starting up and implementing a council of equals are listed in the table on the following page.

Where autocratic rule has been the norm, it can take participants a long time to test the sincerity of the leadership and the integrity of the new framework. And a council will not really get off the ground until members trust what's going on and give themselves over to the new endeavor. This trust and letting go arises out of having a direct and positive personal experience within the council framework over time. The process can be speeded up by:

• using external consultants and facilitators on occasion in high-leverage ways

Start-up Milestones for a Council of Equals

☐ Formal leader decides to establish a council of equals, and at least one other person willingly joins to form a group.

☐ Group establishes regular meetings and issues minutes.

☐ Group begins to use consensus decision making.

☐ Group develops its mission statement and governing ideas, clarifying the specific responsibilities and boundary conditions of the new council. These are approved by higher-level administration if group is part of a larger organization.

☐ Group develops and completes personal commitment statement and charter to work in good faith per the mission statement and governing ideas. Charter is signed by each member, and countersigned by higher-level administration if group is part of a larger organization.

☐ Group specifies and establishes norms and expectations for member behavior.

☐ Group begins sharing management responsibilities and balancing individual workloads.

☐ Group and individual members complete core training programs as needed.
- problem-solving skills
- interpersonal skills
- team process skills

☐ Group begins periodic assessments on its performance.
- external
- internal

- addressing some of the old baggage and negative feelings if the group has a history
- learning more about individual differences
- conducting training in group process skills
- regarding whatever matters are at hand as raw material for learning and growing together

With good faith effort over time, significant trust develops for the new system and process. Participants become more open to hearing what each other has to say, and more skilled at handling difficult and controversial issues together. They also become increasingly confident that the group can effectively handle whatever arises and needs to be addressed. Nevertheless, in the near term the migration requires extra time and effort in order to: (1) learn new skills, and (2) realign administrative infrastructure for congruency with participatory governance. Regarding the latter, for example, foundational work needs to be done on the governing ideas and the team charter. *Appendix A* provides more information on how to align administrative infrastructure for participatory governance.

With the top-down autocratic framework gone, participants begin to deal with the new reality: the old problem of *the boss* is replaced by the new problem of *ourselves*. Issues of personal growth and peer-level relationships move to the fore. Also, with power and authority distributed more equally, group members feel increasingly responsible when things are dysfunctional. As full partners in co-creating and managing the enterprise, they cannot easily rationalize and blame others for a continuing problem that has not been addressed. People's sense of personal responsibility and integrity therefore naturally build energy toward taking initiative to raise and address outstanding issues.

Without the politics, stress, and emotional baggage endemic in autocratic systems, things get a lot easier as the council matures. Over the longer term, people develop a genuine appreciation for one another and their differences, as well as a sense of ease about the council process. Direct personal experience repeatedly affirms that the best and most satisfying outcomes are the result of a creative coalescing of diverse views and perspectives. Members learn to show up with a personal perspective but unmade-up mind, share all of who and what they are, and trust the process. There is more energy and joy in the group, and more work gets done by more people.

Nevertheless, the journey toward authenticity and mutual understanding has its ups and downs, and often results in confusion, anxiety, discomfort, and doubt. The most difficult things to learn and do in a council are: (1) handle conflict, (2) appreciate and value differences, and (3) hold one another accountable. Interestingly, these same challenges invariably prove to be the most significant opportunities for personal growth and development.

The following chart provides an overview of the different phases and their specific challenges for implementing a council of equals.

Challenges to Implementing a Council of Equals

Phase I

Letting Go and Jumping Off

- *Overcoming Fear*. Formal leaders need to overcome their fear and resistance to giving up unilateral control and power over others.

Phase II

Migrating to the New System

- *Learning New Skills*. People need to learn the group process skills necessary to weave individual differences into a fabric of collective decision making and action.

- *Dealing with Old Baggage*. The legacy of the previous autocratic system will typically include unprocessed negative thoughts and feelings. For leaders to demonstrate their good faith in the new format, they need to be willing to address some of these with the group.

- *Revising Administrative Infrastructure*. How things get done in the new system will require revising old and/or creating new administrative elements, ranging from crafting the governing ideas to changing how performance assessments are done.

- *Building Trust*

- *Being Patient*. All of this takes extra time and effort.

Phase III

Living It Out

- *Trusting the Process*
- *Being Authentic*
- *Handling Conflict*
- *Accepting One Another and Valuing Differences*
- *Holding One Another Accountable*

Advice for Formal Leaders

While the following suggestions apply to all members of a council, they are particularly important for formal leaders working as first among equals in a larger organization or institution.

1. *Be honest and clear.* Do not start a council unless you are called to do so; that is, unless you really want to and are in it for the long haul. Without a true calling or vocation for the work, you will not be able to do it.

2. *Be ready.* Be prepared to: (1) assume personal accountability for the council and its outcomes, and (2) work harder for a while than you have been working.

3. *Be willing to be vulnerable.* Autocratic systems enable leaders to ensconce themselves behind facades of power and position, protected from being openly challenged by others. But the openness and transparency of a council make that impossible. Fortunately, what we choose to hide and defend is rarely part of our higher or better selves. For leaders who are willing to be transparent and vulnerable, the council of equals model provides extraordinary opportunities for personal and professional growth.

4. *Set the right intention.* Make a commitment to balance the legitimate needs of all affected parties in an open and transparent manner. This practice

of *moral symmetry* is the best ground to stand
on for dealing forthrightly and effectively with
whatever arises.

5. *Check the Context.* If the council is part of a larger
   organization, make sure that the administrative
   and cultural environment is generally supportive
   or at least neutral (rather than hostile) regarding
   participatory governance.

6. *Get permission.* Get documented approval from
   executive administration on the governing ideas
   and council charter.

7. *Make it easy on others.* Do not create extra work
   for those you report to or those you serve. The
   openness and transparency of the council should
   make things easier for them, not more difficult.

8. *Use connective technologies.* New technologies—
   including email, texting, tweeting, social
   networking, online meetings, and You
   Tube—enable council members to interact
   and collaborate in extraordinary ways on a
   real-time basis. Use them to handle emergent
   issues, maintain ongoing communication
   related to matters at hand, keep meetings free
   and clear of clutter, and better connect with
   your stakeholders.

9. *Continue your own growth and development.*
   Our capacity to respond to life—rather than

react—depends on who we are and have become. So continued learning and development are incredibly important. Dedicate yourself to becoming the best that you can be. Regard *everything* that arises as raw material for that journey. Establish a spiritual practice and discipline if you do not already have one (e.g., centering prayer, yoga, nature-based awareness practices, meditation). Review secular development programs you're already familiar with and explore new ones. Check out some of those listed in *Appendix B*. Take to heart the ones that resonate for you. Question and challenge yourself with them. Have fun with them. Hold yourself accountable for bringing them alive as a way of being.

10. *Avoid factions in the group.* To maintain group integrity, coalitions and factions need to be discouraged and avoided. Members can do this by: (1) being honest and open-minded in discussions, (2) refraining from aligning support for positions outside the group meetings, and (3) trusting that the group process is an opportunity to create something better than what could be created otherwise.

11. *Get help.* If possible, use external facilitators, consultants, and coaches when needed. But be discerning: you need wise and capable individuals to help you sustain and nurture this kind of enterprise. If funding is an issue,

discuss it with these people and ask for a discounted rate. The best ones will gladly make adjustments to support and be engaged with such meaningful work.

12. *Network with others for mutual support.* Get connected with kindred spirits for mutual support and affirmation. One of the best ways to do that is through the *Robert K. Greenleaf Center for Servant Leadership.* There is unlimited potential support and validation for a council of equals within the Servant-Leadership community. See *Appendix B* for more information on the Greenleaf Center and its offerings.

13. *Consider having an advisory committee.* Chosen by the council, the advisory committee would periodically help the group by providing another perspective and being witness to whatever is going on.

14. *Periodically review the governing ideas.* Everything is changing all the time. So it is important to periodically review the governing ideas of the enterprise, including the mission statement, values, goals, and strategies. Do your best to assure that these compass headings point unfailingly in the right direction.

Appendix A

A Checklist for Shared Governance ——————

☐ *Team-based Structure.* The basic organizational unit, whether at the frontline or in the boardroom, is the group or team. Members have a mix of three complementary capacities needed to do the work: (1) technical and functional expertise, (2) problem-solving and decision-making skills, and (3) interpersonal skills related to effective communication and group process. The group operating dynamic is an open forum in which each member freely participates as he or she chooses. Members report to the group as a whole rather than to a single boss or administrator.

☐ *Volition and Choice.* As much as possible, systems and processes are based on free will and choice: no one is coerced into doing something. Decision-making is done by consensus.

☐ *Clarity on Purpose and Boundary Conditions.* The purpose, mission, values, and goals are all clear. Members know their rights and responsibilities. There is a sense of responsible autonomy, in which both the members and the group decide for themselves what to do and are then held accountable for the outcomes.

☐ *Partnership and Influence.* People are partners and collaborators in the enterprise. In the words of one practitioner, this means: "Whatever we're in we both created, and we're both responsible for creating tomorrow." Members have meaningful influence on the group, and the group has influence on the larger system — upwardly, laterally, and downwardly.

☐ *Countervailing Power.* Every person has influence and power. No one person has unilateral power over another. Individuals and the group are able to raise issues and pursue appeals without fear of retribution.

☐ *Alignment of Systems and Processes.* Governance and management functions are accomplished through pluralistic, egalitarian, open-ended exchanges. Processes related to strategies, plans, initiatives, budgets, goals, feedback, and rewards are all determined and accomplished in participatory ways.

☐ *Leadership.* The formal leaders are *firsts among equals* rather than *bosses*. Although they are expected to provide a reckoning on organizational outcomes and are therefore personally at risk, they cannot coerce others to do things they do not want to do. Leaders serve the enterprise as coaches, facilitators, role models (walking the talk), mentors, experts, and partners, thereby helping to create capacity in the group and organization. They hold the enterprise and system in trust as an act of stewardship and service for the greater good.

☐ *Mutual Acceptance and Support.* Everyone matters: the group honors and actively supports the dignity, rights and responsibilities of each member. Each person is accepted and valued for who he or she is. Individuals are thereby supported in being authentic, bringing all of who they are to the group. It is also recognized that both individuals and the group need self-understanding and a wide range of social and technical skills to effectively govern and manage the enterprise. There is, therefore, considerable support for personal and professional development.

☐ *Openness and Transparency.* The system is an open book: there are no secrets. Information about revenue, income, expenses, performance, salaries, merit pay, and other business metrics is readily available. Processes and decisions are handled aboveboard and involve those affected as well as those who will have to make things work.

Appendix B

Resources and References _____

As much as I like one-stop shopping, I confess that this handbook does not include all that you need to know for implementing a council of equals. It covers the basics, but there is a lot more that would be of help to you on the journey. Following are some of the sources that helped me. My guess is they will help you, too, if you are going to do something like this. But do not be turned off if some of them seem dated or appear parochial: after all, wisdom is timeless and comes in myriad forms.

Books on Council Practice

> *Facilitator's Guide to Participatory Decision-Making* by Sam Kaner (Josey-Bass). The very best book and resource available on collaborative problem solving and group decision making. A treasure trove of practical concepts, innovative tools, and creative methods. Not just highly recommended: indispensable. (*Note:* Material from this book was adapted and used herein for the section on *Meetings and Gatherings.*)

> *Consensus: A New Handbook for Grassroots Political, Social and Environmental Group* by Peter Gederloos (See Sharp Press). An excellent and practical guide to consensus decision making. (*Note:* Material from this book was adapted and

used for the sections on *Consensus* and *Meetings and Gatherings*.)

The Way of Council by Jack Zimmerman and Virginia Coyle (Bramble Books). A comprehensive manual that includes helpful information on council forms, practices, listening skills, and leadership issues, along with specifics for using councils in families, schools, and businesses. Recommended for those who want to explore council as a way of life. (*Note:* Material from this book was adapted and used for the section on *Confidentiality*.)

Building United Judgment: A Handbook for Consensus Decision Making by the Center for Conflict Resolution. (*Note:* Material from this book was adapted and used for the section on *Supportive Conditions*.)

Readings on Leadership

"The Servant as Leader" and "The Institution as Servant" by Robert K. Greenleaf. Insightful essays calling for a more caring society and participatory approach to leadership. The latter essay includes a succinct and powerful summary on the drawbacks of top-down autocratic governance. Available through the Robert K. Greenleaf Center for Servant-Leadership at www.greenleaf.org.

"Holistic Servant-Leadership" by George SanFacon and Larry Spears *(The Spears Center for Servant-Leadership)*. Essay outlining a holistic leadership model and map that includes the council of equals. Printed copies are available through *The Spears Center for Servant-Leadership*. Also available free online at www.spearscenter.org.

Systems of Organization: Management of the Human Resource by David Bowers (University of Michigan Press). This classic text powerfully and succinctly outlines the comparative effectiveness of different governance systems, from authoritarian to participatory. (*Note:* The section on *Participation in Practice* was excerpted and adapted from this book.)

A Conscious Person's Guide to the Workplace, George SanFacon (Trafford Publishing). A compendium and resource for creating workplaces and organizations that evoke and engage the human spirit. For readers who want to know more about the philosophy and worldviews that underpin participatory governance and the council of equals.

Programs for Growth and Development

Community at Work "Facilitation Training." *Community at Work* is a think tank and consulting firm dedicated to "building models of group collaboration and putting them into practice." Their acclaimed workshops — *Leader as Facilitator* and *Group Facilitation Skills*—are probably the best available trainings on collaborative problem solving and group decision making.

The Seven Habits of Highly Effective People. An excellent personal development program in the art of living, based upon Stephen Covey's book of the same name (Free Press). Structured around a few simple repeated behaviors, this program helps people to put their own psychological house in order and provides excellent guidelines for group interaction. Certified trainers offer and teach on-site programs, but they are expensive. As an alternative, people can simply use the book and available learning materials (including CDs and DVDs) to work through the material, either individually and/or in concert with one another.

Dialogue. A powerful social technology for having difficult conversations that address complex, controversial, and important issues. I have read several books on dialogue but it is best learned by simply doing it, whereby an experienced facilitator leads a group through dialogic conversations interspersed with some theory. Just a few in-depth sessions can get a group up and running.

Myers-Briggs Temperament Styles. A Jungian approach to personality typing. Great material for developing a deeper understanding and genuine appreciation of both ourselves and

others. The book I am most familiar with is
*Please Understand Me II: Temperament, Character,
and Intelligence* by David Keirsey (Prometheus
Nemesis Book Company). It provides both theory
and application material, including a personal
survey instrument to help determine your
particular temperament type. The instrument is
also available online at www.keirsey.com.

*Loving What Is: Four Questions That Could
Change Your Life*, by Byron Katie (Harmony
Books). A powerful and simple method of self-
inquiry known as *The Work*. The process entails
identifying, questioning, and turning around
negative thinking, the source of much needless
suffering in the world. See Katie's website for
more information and learning materials at www.
thework.com.

Challenge Ropes Courses. An outdoor personal
development and team building activity
consisting of low elements (close to the ground)
and high elements (using trees and/or man-made
structures). Programs are designed to confront
personal fears and self-imposed limits, and to
explore group interaction and problem-solving
skills. A great experience for any group—from
work teams to families—to share. Check your
local neighborhood for a course and program
near you.

Networking

Robert K. Greenleaf Center for Servant Leadership. A non-profit organization that provides resources and opportunities to explore the practice of servant leadership with others. Offerings include an annual conference, information on best practices, related books and video-based training materials, and myriad networking opportunities. There is unlimited potential support and validation for a council of equals within the servant-leadership community. Learn more at www.greenleaf.org.

Acknowledgements ————————

Thanks to…

—those who lived out the way of council with me in the workplace, especially: Roy Christian, Ken Davis, Vicky Hueter, Joe Kennedy, and Jeff Schroeder

—those who supported us in doing that, especially: Barb Cecil of *The Ashland Institute*; Ginny Gilmore of *The Sophia Foundation*, Bernadette Malinoski of *Workplace Partners*; Anita Zimmerman and John DeSouza of *Interax*; staff and the community at *The Robert K. Greenleaf Center for Servant Leadership*; and executive administrators at *The University of Michigan*

—Roann Altman and Dorothy Lenz, editors and compadres extraordinaire, for their help and support on early drafts of the manuscript

—my son, Alex, for the cover art and book layout

—my friend Hal Rothbart at *Charing Cross Press* for his publishing expertise and support

—my mentors and guides: Jaguar, Bill Bottum and Arthur Pendragon, for calling me to do this work and then supporting me in doing it

With love and gratitude,

George

About the Author

Photo courtesy of John Noble

George has worked as a grocery clerk, painter, maintenance mechanic, custodian, security guard, high school teacher, short-order cook, facilities engineer, energy conservation consultant, trainer, facilitator, operations director, management consultant, and executive coach. While an administrator at *The University of Michigan*, he helped pioneer and implement a participatory approach to management and governance—the council of equals—that was nationally recognized for its innovation and effectiveness.

George is author of *A Conscious Person's Guide to the Workplace* and *Adventures in Healing* (both available through Amazon.com), and co-author of the essay, *Holistic Servant-Leadership* (available free online at www.spearscenter.org).

He lives and works as a part-time caretaker at a homestead in southern Michigan. He also devotes time to environmental stewardship of the surrounding lakes and woodlands, and to promoting servant leadership. George can be reached via email at gasanfan@umich.edu.